Malan Wright

Pages from the sermons of a young country minister

Malan Wright

Pages from the sermons of a young country minister

ISBN/EAN: 9783337124649

Printed in Europe, USA, Canada, Australia, Japan

Cover: Foto ©Suzi / pixelio.de

More available books at **www.hansebooks.com**

PAGES FROM THE SERMONS

of a

OUNG COUNTRY MINISTER.

PAGES FROM THE SERMONS

∴ of a ∴

YOUNG COUNTRY MINISTER.

To My Mother,

My guardian, companion, and friend in childhood, youth,
and manhood, I affectionately dedicate
this little book.

THE AUTHOR.

FAITH.

THOUGH days and months and years I bear
    A cross of wood,
    Though bend with care,
. Though grief o'er all my life be spread;
If faith be absent, I am dead.

Faith only is the living stay
Of living men along the way.
The law my guide, I start and shrink;
But walk with faith along the brink:
And sorrow ne'er can darker be
Than faith shall light the way for me.
She rides in peace above the wave;
She knows her God is strong to save.

CALVARY.

WHAT sage research had never found;
    What nature never knew;
What cries and tears could not avail,
    Is offered free to you.

Man labors on from youth to age,
    Perplexed with various care;
Though strain and toil be multiplied,
    His sin shall yet be there.

The troubled conscience seeks for peace;
    She tries full many a road:
Yet, though her feet be tired and sore,
    She leadeth not to God.

There is one Way and only one—
    All others go astray—
Since thou dost know it, travel on;
    Begin in it to-day.

It is "The way of holiness;"
    O'er it go no unclean:
Warfaring men and fools as well,
    They shall not err therein.

No lions there nor rav'nous beast;
    They shall not there be found;
But the redeemed shall walk therein;
    Their peace and joy abound.

THE "MORNING STAR."

HE SPAKE! the mountains firmly stood,
　The valleys and the crystal flood;
The sun shone out with golden light;
The moon led forth the starry night.

He spake! and man alone appeared,
And viewed the scene his Lord had reared:
In lovely guise and modest mien,
The partner of his joys is seen.

Alas, that joy should be so brief!
Departing as the falling leaf!
Some bitter spell, foul sin hath found;
And hope is fallen to the ground.

But, sure, there doth a star arise!
It beams in *Abel's* sacrifice!
This star of hope shall never set;
It glows, and beams, and brightens, yet.

Where is its orbit? Whence doth shine
This beaming star, so much Divine?
From Calvary's cross it lights afar,
Forward and *backward*—glorious star!

Its gleaming light shall never set,
A light for weary pilgrims, yet;
And children's children, from afar,
Shall hail with joy the "Morning Star."

A PRAISE LYRIC.

Bring hither all your garlands now,
   And wreath them for Immanuel's brow :
The honors richest, brightest, best,
Forever on His head shall rest.

Stoop down and touch the trembling lyre:
Kindle each voice with passion's fire:—
No strains so sweet shall ever be
As the saved render, Lord, to thee.

Why is it that they tarry,
   And press not to the van—
Behind, the cross of Calv'ry;
   Before, the dying man?

WISDOM.

There is a wisdom sure and true;
   A wisdom old yet ever new:
No price can gain it; it is free:—
Thy God would grant it, man, to thee.

Before it dwindles human lore;
It is since all and was before—
Listen, O man! it calls to thee:
Heed thou its voice—'twill make thee free.

LUKE X: 2.

HARVESTS on harvests plenteous
  Reapers and laborers few;
Room waiting—fields of whiteness—
  The call is made to you.

Say not you are not able
  To gather in a sheaf—
The grain falls out and wasteth;
  The harvest time is brief.

Work while the day time lasteth;
  The night fast draweth nigh:
The faithful laborer laboreth;
  The fruit, laid up on high.

And when the fields of whiteness
  Stretch out before our view;
While, throughout all their borders,
  The laborers are few;

The old command before us,
  Calls to the place of prayer;
That He Who loves the harvest,
  May send the laborers there.

ONLY TRUST HIM.

THEY who trust Him shall rejoice;
He's the best, the only choice:
Choose Him, He will bring you home—
Choose Him while there yet is room.

In the grave no choice is made,
Passed the grain under the blade:
Be it tare or be it wheat,
Each lies for its own place meet.

Never will the reaper there
Change to wheat the gathered tare:
Soul of sin, and soul of grace—
Each shall go to its own place.

Enter then, there yet is room,
E'er the darkness of the tomb;
Enter while the light of day
Calls you from your sins away.

HEAVEN.

O HEAVEN indeed thou dearest place!
　　What storms of earth so fierce,
　　　　Or dark, or swift, or terrible,
　　The hope of thee to pierce?

Rejoicing in the hope of thee,
　　And looking for thy light,
　　　　How can we see the clouds that rise
　　To hide thy glory bright?

Earth's hopes grow dim and disappear;
　　Earth's sweetest fruits may cloy:
　　　　But hope of Heaven's futurity,
　　Has bliss without alloy.

Real for unreality;
　　The substance for the shade;
　　　　The fruit after the very storm
　　That watered well the blade.

INVITATION.

COME while mercy sheds its ray,
  Bright with hope, on life's short day—
  Day that soon must pass away,
  Leaving naught but crumbling clay.

  Then the harvest may be past;
  Then the door of hope be fast.
  Many then shall stand aghast
  In that awful day, the last.

  Come while life is fair and bright:
  Choose the path of truth and right;
  Way that runs and ends in light;
  Leads to beatific sight.

  Night there is without, and gloom;
  Yet within the kingdom room—
  Heaven and rest and endless home:
  Hither, wanderer! enter, come.

"Truly our fellowship is with the Father, and with His Son Jesus Christ."
—1 *John*, 1: 3.

ETERNAL fellowship of love;
  Begun on earth, complete above:
  Nor earth, nor air, nor rolling sea,
  Can find the soul such company.

What else can satisfy its life?
Who else can nerve it for the strife?
Or what can feed the hungry heart,
If it from Christ, its Bread, depart?

Yet where doth beam this Heavenly Sun?
Upon the lowly contrite one:
And he who trembleth at the word
Of Zion's King, in reverence heard,

Shall find his soul glad company,
The eternal, sacred, holy Three:
For God in glory shall abide
Within the hearts that thus provide.

A PRAYER.

O JESUS, my Saviour,
    In th' depth of thy grace
Oh! show me thy favor—
    Oh! show me thy face.

Thy mercy is gracious;
    Thy name, it is love—
Oh! grant me thy pardon,
    And help from above.

I long time have wander'd
    In darkness and sin—
Oh! enter my heart's door,
    And cleanse me within.

Though I were the foulest,
    Thy blood can make clean:
Thy death was for sinners;
    On thee will I lean.

Rejoice, O my soul, thou;
    His mercy is sure:
Though diseased, thou shalt find there
    An infinite cure.

His smile, it is health, then;
    His love, it is peace;
From all of sin's tossings,
    A happy release.
            —Amen.

WILL you not choose His path to-night?
His service is the way of light:
His kingdom is the Heavenly place,
The home of all the heirs of grace.

So darksome is earth's brightest day!
So long and rough the shortest way!
So filled with gloom its gathering night,
When here we only walk by sight!

Still shines on earth the Morning Star—
Effulgence streaming from afar—
It guideth to the home of rest,
The mansions of the ever-blest.

Follow its light—make it thy guide—
You need no other ray, beside—
'Twill lead thee to the perfect day;
'Twill cast a halo o'er the way.

LIKE God would ye be?
    Then value the days
When the lot of the downcast
    Ye may lighten with praise;
When lap of the hungry
    Ye may fill full with wheat:
And the pale, starveling children
    May strengthen with meat.

Search out the widow;
    Bring *hope* to her breast;
And nourish the fatherless
    Out of your best.
Try, break off the strong chains
    From the captives of sin;
And shelter the homeless
    Your own home within.

Like God would ye be?
    Then up and be strong;
Improve the bright talents
    That to thee belong:
Bring into the store-house
    Of glad heavenly love,
Such rich, golden treasures
    As cause joy above.

CHARITY.

CHARITY is a wonderful thing.
Such is the feathering over her wing,
Mantle she makes so great as shall hide
Like to the coverings of the salt tide.

Shame finds a garment wonderful fair;
Poverty hides there and loses her care;
Sin comes with weeping under that wing;—
Charity is a most beautiful thing.

Look thee within—has thy soul any wing?
Or chief in its building is there a sting?
Dark is the storm that earth overcasts;
Shelter thee some from the withering blasts.

Is it a foe? Yet bid him come in—
Foemen are sufferers, also, from sin:
Lovest thou God? Then like Him must be;
Thou wast God's enemy—Christ died for thee.

Over the depth of our sin and our shame,
Love is the messenger sent to reclaim;
Hush then the voice of thy clamoring spite—
Lovest thou only the one who does right?

" Weep o'er the erring one," lift him with prayer
Into the realm of the Father's own care;
Seek to reclaim him, but never with spite—
Thou art the one who not always dost right.

Love is a virtue so deep and so high
It must descend to us out of the sky;
Earth cannot nurture it—earth is too dry—
This plant must be watered out of the sky.

HARK to the voice of love Divine;
  Drive forth His enemy and thine;
Purge all thy soul from thoughts unkind;
And fill thee with a Heavenly mind.

Let all thy actions drop with love;
Choose for thy pattern God above;
Be Christ-like in humility;
Be man-like in docility.

"Hitherto Hath the Lord Helped Us."

———

THIS "hitherto" demands our praise
Throughout the remnant of our days:
Demands the high and swelling song
To roll through all our lives along:
Demands a life so pure and good,
'Twill be for other lives as food.

This hitherto—'tis great and high;
Its mercies reach unto the sky:
And time's too short to sing its praise:—
Heaven's ages will the anthem raise.

Wake, then, the song; its voice shall be
An echoing voice of joy to thee.
Begin that praise so deep and high
Thou'lt finish it beyond the sky.
There with angelic hosts above,
Join thou to praise *redeeming love.*

RISE, then, ye hosts against our Lord;
    Put on your eager boast:
We meet you not with trumpet loud,
    Nor million-throated host.

We call not earth and air to fight,
    Nor shiv'ring hail to fall:
The church while battling for the right,
    Relies more on the call—

Lord send thy Spirit from above,
    " In plenitude of grace;"
Convert thine enemies in love,
    And save th' apostate race.

SOWING.

SOW with a lavish hand;
    Sow early and with toil:
Sow when the evening comes apace;—
    No seeds in faith sown spoil.

They shall be treasure cast
    Like bread the waters o'er;
They shall spring up, fruit of the past,
    And springing, bless thee more.

God rules in the desert
  Where the voice of man is still,
He rules in the crowded city;
  But *here* no rebel-will
Opposes its dark designs
  To the will of Him who made it;
But as, in our northern pines
  Ere the foot of man invaded,
There was quiet, and peace, and rest;
  So the lonely peaks of Sinai
Obeyed their King's behest.

Alone with God, Elijah,—
  It is well indeed for thee;
But would it have been, poor sinner,
  For thy soul and for me?

Discouraged art thou, and weary?
  The angel of hope may come;
And, touching thee with his finger,
  Feed thee and spur thee on.

But, remember! God's good angels
  Come not to rebellious souls;
And would'st thou see the water,
  And the cake baked on the coals?

Enlist thee under the banner
    Of Him who has died to save;
Then the angels shall minister to thee,
    Or fellowship over the grave.

Worn out with thy earthly endeavor,
    There'll be bread for thee from above,
And the gentle touch of the angel,
    And the ministry of love.

Oh! yes, there is friendship sweeter,
    And fellowship richer far;
For God will be thy Companion,
    And thy joy earth cannot mar.

—   —

L ET us sanctify through the word of God and praye
every creature of God's hand which He bestow
upon us. So shall our days be passed in the fea
and love of God.

    Not lightly with unfeeling mirth
    Let us enjoy the gifts of earth;
    Not thoughtless, as if all below
    Were here to stay nor we to go:

    But reverent, thankful, full of love
    Toward God who reigns below, above;
    With hearts of tenderness and zeal
    To seek each one the others weal.

IVE me Jesus in my soul—the effects of His salvation received through faith—and I despise all of earth's philosophies, traditions, cultures. I know that they are but cold, shallow, though pretentious things. They may affect the external. They cannot give life. They cannot give pardon of sin—never—never—never. They cannot form the heart in Godlike likeness—never, never. They cannot restore God to His righful place in the soul and its affections—never, never. They cannot move the soul to *love* for its fellow men—never.

They are shadowy forms that *seem* to be;
But their seeming can never change the me
That lies beneath the outward sight,
The *I* that should and must do right.

There are things that *promise* that they are good,
There are dainties that claim to be living food;
But when tried of the soul they are evil found—
The soul that eats them returns to the ground.

The promise of life they do not fulfill.
Oh! follow them, starving man, if you will:
But know that, when time shall cease to be,
Dry dust and ashes they'll be to thee,

Hateful things with a promise that lies;
The soul that feeds upon them dies.

THE Bread I covet most
  Is not the moulding loaf;
The earthy wheat though fair and bright,
  Is not for me enough.

There is a Heaven-giv'n loaf,
  A life-giving supply;
Sinners may eat, be satisfied;
  May feed, and never die.

Its cost a painful cross,
  The agony of Heaven;
Such cost 's above our highest price :—
  It must be freely giv'n.

Freely? Yes. 'tis the word
  Jehovah writes in blood;
Come, take, and thou shalt surely live,
  Upon the word of God.

Reject not such a love;
  Scorn not compassion high:—
Rejecting, there's a vast remove;
  He that rejects must die.

There *is* a way from out
  The curse of broken law;—
A curse for us hath Christ been made;—
  Prophets the promise saw.

Oh! then, my soul, rejoice;
    Thou hast a Priest above:
"His hands are made of tenderness;
    His heart is made of love."

He is the sacrifice,
    And He the offerer, too.
Such love endures through endless years;
    Such love is ever new.

To-day it is the same
    As when on Calvary's brow
A weary sufferer bore the cross—
    O. man! receive it now.

GOD is a rock. Not a rock like a rock of our earth—hardened from boiling liquid, and in God's good time to return again by fire to boiling mass and then to volatile gas; but a "rock of ages"—

Before the ages of earth began,
And after the coming of creature man;
And after the ages of earth shall cease,
And strife of nations shall end in peace.

How blest the child whose early steps
    Are guided in Thy truth,
Whose feet pursue the path divine,
    E'en in the days of youth.

Manhood with all its care and strife
    Shall press his soul in vain;
He knows the path of endless life,
    Nor chooses death again.

Old age shall blossom on his head;—
    He still Thy truth pursues:
The world with all that it can boast,
    Hides not the Heav'n he views.

Oh! blessed, then, the early train'd
    In paths of God's own truth;
They walk in Heav'n's own light and peace,
    Up to old age, from youth.

"FOR HE CARETH FOR·YOU."

LIFE is like a summer sea;
 Sailing, floating, loving, we;
 Skies of brightness o'er us bend;
 All around us seems a friend.

 Life is like a wintry tide,
 Rocks and wintry shores descried;
 Beating waves with freezing crest,
 Heart of mariner distressed.

 But above both smile and frown,
 There's a voice that's not our own—
 Voice that with a right good will,
 Said on Galilee, " Be still."

 Trust we, then, the voice above,
 Voice of mercy, voice of love;
 Cast we all our burning care
 At the feet of Jesus there.

PRAYER MEETING.

LET us improve our opportunities,
    Fast flitting away;
Ending some morrow,
    It may be to-day;

Bearing themselves
    Down the swift flowing stream;
Ending so suddenly,
    Like to a dream.

Mercy is calling us;
    Love still says come:
Christ is yet waiting
    To give us a home.

Blessings of earth
    Still speak of the love
Pouring upon us
    From the Father above.

Still unbelief,
    With snare and with wile,
Lurketh about us
    To trap and beguile.

While it's about us
  To lure and destroy,
While sins within us
  O'er-power and annoy,

Meet we together,
  And oft in one place
Speak to each other
  The word of God's grace.

———

THIS lone "monk," (Luther) as his emperor called
him, was to inflict a humbling blow upon the
papacy.

Not cohorts armed in glittering steel,
  Not bugle throated host,
Not council grand from every land,
  Nothing for man's brave boast.

Alone, with God above:
  Alone, with God around:
Mid fiercest bands and iron hands,
  A trusting soul was found.

DEATH.

―――

"Flowers have their time to fade;"
    "Leaves have their time to fall;"
The spring nurses the tender blade;
    Ripens the fruits, the tall.

But all times are thine own,
    O, thou stern reaper, Death;
Bright youth, old age, and manhood's prime,
    The infant's gentle breath.

Thou lay'st thy hand upon
    The beating heart of youth;
Thou leavest beauty on the brow,
    But life is gone, in truth.

The cold, the marble clay
    Is but the *form* we loved;
The soul has fled us quite away,
    Nor lips for us will move.

All times are thine, O Death;
    I may not call my own
A single moment that I live:
    It may be thine alone.

BUILDING WELL.

GOD stops us in the race of time
And shows some things are true.
The things we pass so lightly by
Abide forever and for aye:

While what engrosses all our thought,
The things we sell, the what we bought,
Pass quick away, though new.

Oh! let us ever learn to prize
The soul that deep within us lies;
And fashion all our use of time
By that, th' immortal and sublime.

While faithful to the lesser trust,
Let us remember we are dust,
A breath that passeth swift away,
A shadow born but not to stay.

Thus may we build on things above
A life of use because of love,
A soulful life wherein the rest
Are made subservient to the best.

May Jesus be our corner-stone,
We build our lives on Him alone;
And every stone through Him be true,
He building and the Builder, too.

MY CHOICE.

WOULD rather sit in the dust below
 With God's sunlight of grace around
Than far above on a lofty throne
 Where God were never found.

I would rather weep in Ramah
 If God be there beside,
Than feast with mirth in Beulah
 Without my Heavenly Guide.

I love the mountain sunlight,
 The bracing of its air;
But better with God in the valley
 Than alone on the hill-top there.

I am not blind to beauty,
 Nor deaf to words of praise:
But, if these beckon me from duty,
 I can wait till the end of days.

For my King will come in splendor,
 In a glory all unknown;
And for every faithful warrior,
 His praise and His lofty throne.

Earth's triumphs are short and fitful:
 Earth's praises feeble and faint:
But oh! for the triumph of Heaven,
 And the Master's praise to His saint!

THE day of light and gladness
    Comes beaming o'er the hills:
It quickens earth's dark madness;
    It melts the frozen rills.

The Sun so long expected,
    The Light of every land,
Shines o'er the towering mountains;
    And falls on every strand.

Throw open wide the shutters
    That hide men from its light;
Remove the human dungeons
    That keep men still in night.

Proclaim in every valley,
    The earth's bright Sun is risen;
And call to all the fettered,
    Come forth from out your prison.

Be slow to cast a shadow
    To hide the risen Lord;
For lo! He comes with angels,
    Bringing to each reward.

Happy, if in that moment,
　　He say to thee, " Well done;"
And with th' attending angels,
　　Declare thy race well run.

But, oh! unspoken sadness
　　If in that hour of fate,
Thy life a faithless fabric,
　‵　He say to thee, " Too late."

———

WHITHER, ah! whither shall I go
　When, quitting this fond world below,
　　I stretch my wings and fly away ?

Whither, oh! whither shall I rest
When, rudely pushed from the home nest,
　I try my wings, so long untried ?

REDEMPTION.

Come tempest wrecked and lost;
Behold the matchless cost
To which thy God hath been
To save thee from despair.

Thy soul so much His care,
Thy soul so great in worth,
The realms of Heavenly bliss
Were robbed to purchase this.

From the blissful realms of day,
See thy Saviour wend His way;
From the throne and glory bright,
From the realms of perfect light,
To the earth shrouded in gloom,
To the cross and to the tomb.

Lift, O Earth, thy highest praise;
Anthems, loud, with angels raise:
Pæans sing with one accord;—
Christ is Saviour, Christ is Lord.

Bethl'ms manger, lowly place,
Speaks thy Saviour's matchless grace;
And the sea of Galilee
Tells of all His love to thee.

Yet of all, divinest spot,
Fills the law in every jot,
Calvary with darken'd sky,
And His wailing, bitter cry.

Here in anguish, sinner, come;
Here behold thy awful doom:
Here behold the Son of God
Laid beneath the awful rod.

O my sins! accursed things!—
Fly from me on swiftest wings.
Christ hath borne my sins; shall I
Add the sins that made him die?

Yet my hope is in His cross;—
All my righteousness is dross;
All my hopes must faint and die
Till beneath His cross I lie.

O divinest, dearest hope,
Thou alone with fears must cope;
Thou alone canst bring the day
To my heart, sin chased away.

Light of all the earth arise;
Bring the day to darkened eyes:
In the dungeons of the blind,
In the depths of clouded mind.

Then shall glory shine afar ;
Light, earth's darkness cannot mar:
All pours forth from one bright Star,
Seen in Bethlehem, seen afar.

Day of hope—its coming dawns—
Prophets sang it ere the morn ;
Yet the day earth waits to see,
Star of hope, O Christ, is Thee.

PROVIDENCE.

THE skill of men and friends all nigh;
  Pillowed on the most downy bed,
  With love and luxury o'erspread—
  One vital spark, all cannot bring;
  We live or die, for God is King.

BE faithful in thy lot:
  Thou knowest surely not
  Whether, amid the pain,
  Waiting for joy again,
  Thy God doth thee prepare
  For some more regal care.

  To-day stand in thy place;
  Fill it with suited grace:
  To-morrow thou canst leave
  To that Hand that doth weave
  For each a destiny
  He giveth not to see.

THEN *let us live in the faith of Jesus,* in full assurance
of hope, looking toward the time of our death with
joy and not with grief; filling up our lives by God's
grace with faithful serving of Christ, the Lord;
looking forward to the great reward to be received
from Christ, our Captain, our sacrifice and our
Priest, our King and our God.

Heaven's high arches then shall ring
When the sheaves we homeward bring;
When poor sinners turn and say,
"Christ has saved my soul to-day."

Oh! if joy in Heaven is found
More o'er one saved soul than ground
Full with rich and plenteous yield
Of the blessings of the field,

Shall we not amid our toil
In the mill and in the soil,
Ever labor to the end
Some poor soul should find its Friend?

Glad, if Christ our spirits fill,
Shall we press to do His will.
Oh! sweet will of God to save!
Likeness to it may we have.

O CALVARY, thou dearest spot!
　　Yet who would ever thought
To find beside its glory there,
　　This sweet " forget-me-not."

A mother's love enshrined within
　　The heart that loveth all:
A son's kind care for mother's weal,
　　Before the dark death pall.

O Son of God! true Son of man!
　　We come of thee to learn
The full glory of righteousness,
　　For which some hearts still yearn.

The cross teaches us sacrifice;—
　　It teaches love of God:
It points the way of life and hope,
　　For those beneath the rod.

" Woman, behold thy son," He said—
　　The angels wondering view—
The glad new day is ushered in:
　　God will make all things new.

New, yes; a new, new righteousness;
    A fuller love to men;
A righteousness so pure and good,
    Beyond the world's short ken.

Glad, earth takes up the loving cry
    Where e'er the cross is found;
Truth springs from out the earth again;
    And goodness, from the ground.

True love of God, pure love to man,
    In Calvary have their rise;
And so old earth is new again,
    Waiting for Paradise.

PRAISE.

EACH morning with its mellow light,
  Each closing day enwrapped in night,
  Each noon-tide meal though simple, quite,
  May find praise add to its delight.

His goodness great unto the cloud that hangs abov
    our head,
  Is surer than the daily bread with which we're fee
  His wonderful surpassing works of grace that o'e
    us pour,
  Are our sure pledge of blessings yet untried, b
    which we ask for more.

Oh! trust His goodness yet my soul, indeed;
Since in the past, in many a sorest need,
Thou hast His goodness tried, and found it sure
While thou hadst naught but praise to render Him
    thou wast so poor.

Wilt thou not then confess before thy fellow me
There is a goodness high above our ken
That deigns in wondrous works His creature
    wants to supply,
And in their time of need is nigh?

Hunger and thirst and homeless wandering sore,
Dark shadows of the dungeon op'ning never mor
Sickness with death-shade on the brow,
Highest and roughest seas before our prow—

All these are nothing to that love,
O man of sin! that seeks thee from above.
Life's wrecks are oft the trysting place
Where God meets man with wondrous grace.

EFORE the day of vengeance falls,
Shelter thee 'neath the eternal walls
Of Zion's city, large and fair; —
Zion's Deliverer welcomes there.

All day His hands are stretched;
And "Come" is the sweet word that bids thee home
Unto thy Father's house of love,
Built here on earth and built above; —
For God's own watchful, loving care
Is with his children everywhere.

———

Acts 2:4.

o seek of God that baptism, divine;
  Let it fill all thy soul.
Then shall thy peace and joy
    Be without end,
When God's best blessing,
His own self,
    Thy paths attend.

Go seek that blessing—'tis the better part;
Come, ask thy Father for it as thou art:
He'll not despise thy humble, contrite prayer;
Thy God Himself will make thy cause His care.

THANKSGIVING DAY, 1885.

———

LET the vales of healthful breath,
Full of life and not of death;
Let the plains where breezes play,
Sweet and pure, the livelong day,
Join with us in songs of praise;
Join in gladsome, thankful lays.

On the air glad life is borne,
Be it zephyr, be it storm;
Hide we not from baleful breath,
Luring us to speedy death.
O ye breezes, wake the song;
Help us praise the whole day long.

No lowing herds are in the stall complaining:
No flocks bleat sadly on the hillsides, wanting food:
All join the voice that says, The Lord is good.

From lonely cabin in the forest dreary,
And sod house on the prairie far away,
Voices of praise and gladness rise to-day.

The dwellers in the city, toiling weary,
And watching round the works of many lands;
Blest in the general benediction, sing psalms.

And they that toil in many a weary fact'ry,
Sharing the good that comes from teeming earth,
To-day, to songs of heart devotion, give birth.

None pine, who fear God, from great sea to ocean,
Because the flocks and herds and crops are not;
But everywhere is plenty, mansion and cot.

Only the poor to-day for food are crying—
Always we have these on our right and left.
Who would not help them in their sighing, of
    love 's bereft.

So, nation, favored by the bounteous Giver,
Forget not to pour forth thy meed of praise
To Him who crownest with a goodly portion,
    thy days.

Jesus Our and Earth's Only Hope.

THE day has dawned. 'Tis Jesus,
    The day-star of the dawn;
He is the star of morning,
    And He, the perfect morn.

He is the sun of splendor
    That makes the noontide ray;
And He, the orb of glory
    That gilds the closing day.

All earth is dark without Him:
    Within, without, around,
In earth, and air, and Heaven,
    No light elsewhere is found.

The heart in its repining
    Mourns for the hoped-for day;
Yet there is naught to light us
    Within our cumbrous clay.

But if, upon our sorrow,
　　His shadow but arise,
The soul, in hope and gladness,
　　Wakes to a new surprise.

Henceforth, earth is His service
　　Who sets the prisoner free;
And life, a joyful anthem
　　Of praise, O Christ, to thee.

———

A WARNING.

———

Not every road runs skyward;
　　Some run to foul despair:
Not every one 's a victor;
　　Some are the conquered there.

THE ATONEMENT.

No bloody rite of mitred priest,
  No life of spotless, harmless beast,
  Washes for us our sin away.

No *less* for us can aught suffice;
  Our sin demands no *less* a price:
  But once for us a Saviour died.

Him, spotless beast but typified;
  And He Himself our Priest appears,
  And quells for us our guilty fears.